INVESTIGATING

the leisure and tourism industries

INVESTIGATING

the leisure and tourism industries

JOHN COLCLOUGH

PROJECT MANAGER: JOHN EDMONDS
PROJECT CONSULTANT: DEBBIE BETTERIDGE

Hodder & Stoughton

A MEMBER OF THE HODDER HEADLINE GROUP

British Library Cataloguing in Publication Data

Colclough, John
  Investigating the leisure and tourism industries. – (Hodder
  GNVQ. Leisure & tourism in action)
  1. Tourist trade   2. Leisure industry
  I. Title
  338.4'791

ISBN 0 340 65835 5

First published 1996
Impression number   10 9 8 7 6 5 4 3 2 1
Year   1999   1998   1997   1996

Typeset by Wearset, Boldon, Tyne and Wear.
Printed in Great Britain for Hoder Educational, a division of Hodder Headline Plc,
338 Euston Road, London NW1 3BH by Bath Press

Contents

Assessment matrix   vi
Acknowledgements   vii
Introduction   ix

1 *The structure of the leisure and tourism industries*   1
  Definitions   1
  Who manages the leisure and tourism industries in the UK?   3

2 *The products and services of the leisure and tourism industries*   14
  Travel in time – the historical development of travel, tourism, leisure and
  recreational activity   16
  Products and services   18
  Case study: the National Motor Museum, Beaulieu, Hampshire   20
  Case study: play schemes – the world of children's fantasy   24

3 *The impact of the leisure and tourism industries*   27
  Sustainable tourism   27
  The British Tourist Authority   32

4 *On the crest of a wave? Developing Dover's leisure and tourism industries*   35
  Case study: P&O's European Ferries operation   37
  Case study: the White Cliffs Experience   38
  Case study: the Dover Harbour Board   41

5 *Review of the Unit*   46

Useful addresses   47
Glossary   49
Index   51

Assessment matrix

The tasks which appear in this volume have been devised to generate the Evidence Indicators of each Element of Unit 1: *Investigating the Leisure and Tourism Industries*, part of the Advanced GNVQ (Applied A level) in Leisure and Tourism (1995 specifications). They will also meet the Performance Criteria (PCs) of the Key Skills Elements indicated below. The term 'Key Skills' is used instead of Core Skills throughout, and the Element numbers refer to 1995 specifications.

Students may provide evidence to meet grading criteria through each task. Tasks set in Sections 2, 3 and 4 involve complex activities and are most likely to generate evidence at Distinction level.

Key Skills Hint boxes precede certain tasks to give help and guidance on the particular skill developed through the task.

Tasks	Unit 1	Key Skills		
		Application of Number	**Communication**	**IT**
1 to 8	1.1	3.1, PCs 1 to 3	—	—
9 to 13	1.2 and 1.3	—	3.2, PCs 1 to 5	—
14 to 16	1.4	—	3.1, PCs 1 to 5	—
17	Review of Unit	—	3.3, PCs 1 to 3	3.3, PCs 1 to 6

Acknowledgements

This volume would not have been written without the considerable help and encouragement given by colleagues and students and by the representatives of each of the travel and tourism organisations mentioned in the text. Indeed, I did not once find difficulty in receiving total support from the industry. Vocational courses are about practical experiences and applications, and it is most satisfying to find such support in leisure and tourism.

Special thanks to Tim Dier and his word-processing skills. Also to the following whose colleagues and staff have assisted wherever necessary: David Johnson, Office for National Statistics; Shona McFarlane, the British Tourist Authority; John Potter, Bluebell Railway; Jill Lomer, Thomas Cook Travel Archive; Tim Whittaker, P&O European Ferries; Graham Carter, Montagu Ventures Ltd; Steve O'Connor, Kompan Ltd; Sally Wookey, White Cliffs Experience; Robin Dodridge and Valerie Crimmin, the Dover Harbour Board; Andrew Harding, Norfolk County Council; Renate Dyer, the Dover Tourist Information Centre.

Introduction: Investigating the Leisure and Tourism Industries

Have you ever stopped to consider the incredible diversity of leisure and tourism? Almost everywhere, you will be able to find evidence of the world's single largest employer. This volume seeks to show you how these industries have become among the leading contributors to the UK's economy. You will also be encouraged to find out what your local area has to offer, while building up a thorough understanding of the national and international perspectives of this fascinating business. You will be surprised at just how far people are involved in leisure and tourism. Consider, for example, the popularity of holiday programmes on the TV, or the racks of leaflets, featuring local attractions, to be found whenever you visit a town hall, hotel, exhibition or library. Indeed, how often have you found yourself looking for the local Tourist Information Office sign?

Leisure and tourism use up a great deal of

FIGURE 1.1 *Direction signs for tourist information and other facilities at the East Point Pavilion, Lowestoft, Suffolk.*

available non-working time, and we have to learn to use this availability sensitively and creatively. We shall soon determine in our studies how to choose between the various organisations and facilities who try to persuade us to use their products and services.

Your course in Advanced Leisure and Tourism will, overall, be an adventure into a highly complex but immensely interesting and rewarding area of study. To this, you will be able to bring your own experiences and expertise, and to add your own ideas and thoughts. You may even be able to secure change when you share your research findings with people already involved in the business.

So, where do we start? Our mission is to investigate the leisure and tourism industries. To do so effectively, we first need to define terms, to make a clear distinction between 'leisure' and 'tourism' and to add, in their right places, 'recreation' and 'travel'. Then we shall go on to look at the structure of each industry, how each has developed over time, which products and services each offers and how each impacts on our society.

Throughout the text, you will find case studies to which you can make reference, applying their contexts to your local situation. The choice of case-study material has been designed to focus your thinking on *issues* involved in the leisure and tourism industries as much as on the actual tasks you are invited to undertake. The aim is to raise your awareness, to encourage your first-hand observation and to enable you to apply research techniques to obtain the results that you need and can then use.

The Structure of the Leisure and Tourism Industries

....

K e y   A i m s

Working through this section, you will:

- investigate the **structures** and **scale** of the leisure and tourism industries, using **official statistics**
- understand the **sectors** of the leisure and tourism industries, using actual examples
- look at the **interrelationships** which exist between the various sectors

DEFINITIONS

What exactly is leisure and tourism? Perhaps the best way for you to understand the precise meaning of these two terms is to first of all brainstorm which facilities aimed at leisure and tourism exist in your local area – perhaps to within a radius of 20 km. There are bound to be some.

Leisure activities involve the constructive use of free time or non-working hours. Tourism, on its part, involves the process of travelling to places away from where people normally live and work. Leisure can also involve recreational activity and pursuits, and the idea of tourism is usually included in various aspects of travel. The terms **leisure** and **recreation** and **travel** and **tourism** should exist side by side when you put together your lists of local organisations in Task 1 on page 2.

The *leisure* list in Task 1 is likely to contain those activities which can be undertaken outside normal working hours or time spent on regular household tasks and activities. People who have more free time than they would wish, i.e. the unemployed or underemployed, also have to be considered. *Their* leisure activities might also be separated from the

TASK 1

In small groups, label two large sheets of paper with the headings 'Leisure and recreation' and 'Travel and tourism' respectively.

- Under the 'Leisure and recreation' heading, brainstorm and name local facilities which offer some or all of the following opportunities for public enjoyment and activity: centres for arts and entertainment, sports and physical activities, outdoor pursuits, playgrounds and play schemes, **heritage** sites, and places offering catering, meeting rooms and other accommodations associated with these facilities

- Under the 'Travel and tourism' heading, brainstorm and name local facilities which involve *first* travel activities, such as travel and business-travel agencies, tour operators and principals such as airlines, rail or coach operators, car-hire firms and shipping companies, and *second* tourist activities, such as national or regional tourist boards, tourist-information centres, tourist attractions, guide services, currency exchanges, transport firms and catering and accommodation houses, pubs and restaurants

You will get further ideas for your lists from Section 2 of this book.

time they spend on regular responsibilities in connection with their home or family.

Leisure activities might involve:

- *passive* pastimes such as reading, watching TV or listening to the radio, going to the cinema, theatre or shows, attending functions at museums or sports centres, visiting friends or relatives, organising a dinner party, attending adult-education or night-school classes, and many others
- *active* pastimes such as gardening, decorating, repairing the car, taking part in sport or other physical activities both indoors and outdoors, and many others

What you need to bear in mind is that anyone's leisure activity depends on many factors, for example how much time is available, how much **disposable income** is available, how close to the provision one happens to live, age, health, education, social class, cultural background and how much of a general willingness and ability there is to participate and to use what is available. To get the best out of one's leisure time means that people have to be creative, inventive and positive, and now that we are moving into an age of more and more available time, it really is increasingly vital to challenge people to participate. As a leisure student, you are likely to be expected to show how this can be done.

The *tourism* list is almost as diverse. Most people associate tourism with the process of travelling away somewhere for a shorter or longer period, perhaps staying away from home and undertaking pleasurable experiences as part of the process. Tourism also involves business people. Our increasingly interconnected world relies heavily on business travel, and on people who negotiate trade and enterprise and organise conventions, exhibitions, conferences and trade fairs. Tourist activities might involve:

- going on holiday – looking up and choosing a holiday from the tens of thousands of offerings in company brochures, or planning one's own tour to take in various points of interest. It might involve friends or relatives, or it could include some form of physical activity such as skiing or watching a major spectator sport like the World Cup. Some people hope to learn a new skill from their travel, such as horse riding or archaeology, while others want to sample new **cultures** and customs

- going on business – trying to sell products to new markets by arranging a stand at a major trade fair or exhibition. Or it could involve negotiations at important meetings and conferences, sometimes politically motivated. It could also involve incentive travel offered as a reward for exceptional effort at work, in sales or marketing, or perhaps for inventing a new process at a factory

WHO MANAGES THE LEISURE AND TOURISM INDUSTRIES IN THE UK?

All organisations need **administrative structures** through which they can be effectively managed. Customers expect efficient service from an informed and helpful staff. Who is to deliver this service? You should now refer to the lists you have made of local leisure and tourism organisations and facilities. Think of how they are run and of who is most likely to staff them. Organisations must have staff who are properly and fully trained in those skills which will ensure that, in any and all eventualities, staff will be on hand to offer assistance and guidance. But who is responsible for organising them, who gives out instructions, and who decides on the policies to be followed? Later Units in this course will guide you in a more detailed analysis of these fundamental questions.

The leisure and tourism industries are extensive and complex. However, three sectors can be identified into which these industries fall: **public**, **private** and **voluntary**. Although these three sectors are closely interrelated, we still need to find out which kinds of organisation fit into each sector, and to investigate how each is managed. The **interrelationships** which occur reflect both the use to which the facilities are put and the extent to which they can be provided by both public and private funds working together for mutual benefit. For example, a local coun-

cil might provide a leisure centre out of public funds but then stipulate that that centre be completely financially self-supporting; or a privately owned squash club might be leased for part of the day to local schools; or a major food chain might decide to sponsor the seating arrangements at a publicly owned stadium. Another example of an interrelationship might occur when a local swimming-pool committee, which has always had difficulty in being financially profitable, offers its refreshments contract to outside caterers rather than trying to manage this on its own. This form of **compulsory competitive tendering** by private firms at publicly owned facilities is now standard practice. You might well try to discover such examples of **dual use**, **joint provision** and other partnerships in your area by asking for details at your local council offices.

Facts and figures

As you would expect, large numbers of people are employed in the leisure and tourism business. Figure 1.2 will give you some idea of the numbers employed in the branches shown. The overall trend shows an increase in the numbers employed. This will have significant effects on the industry, and one point indeed is very clear: leisure and tourism are growth industries in the UK.

Much statistical material is published about the leisure and tourism industries which assists people in planning for successful operations. The figures used here are highly selective, and you can obtain more details by writing to one of the addresses given in the 'Useful addresses' section at the end of this volume.

We are mostly concerned with travel and tourism in the UK, and you will appreciate that many foreign visitors help to account for the figures involved here. However, UK residents in turn also travel abroad and spend much money. A comparison of these two sets of statistics is useful – see Figure 1.4.

FIGURE 1.2 *Employment in tourism-related industries in the UK, in 000s.*

	Hotels and other tourist accommodation	Restaurants, cafes etc.	Bars, public houses and nightclubs	Travel agencies/ tour operators	Libraries/ museums other cultural activities	Sport & other recreation activities	All
1994							
Mar	273.9	292.3	350.7	66.5	75.8	305.0	1,364.2
Jun	322.0	313.1	358.2	71.9	78.5	316.5	1,460.2
Sep	332.4	320.8	365.9	72.1	81.6	318.0	1,490.8
Dec	289.7	312.8	366.1	68.0	78.7	302.4	1,417.7
1995							
Mar	292.8	312.3	372.8	69.5	78.3	311.5	1,437.2
Jun	343.9	337.2	383.5	75.2	83.4	324.8	1,548.0
Sep	340.9	338.2	389.3	74.9	83.9	318.3	1,545.3
Changes:							
Sep 1995–1994							
No. (thousands)	8.5	17.4	23.4	2.8	2.3	0.3	54.5
Percentage	2.5	5.4	6.4	3.8	2.8	0.1	3.7

SOURCE: *Labour Market Trends, February 1996, Office for National Statistics.*

T A S K 2

Figures 1.3 and 1.4 opposite demonstrate that significantly more British residents travelled abroad than overseas residents visited the UK. However, the difference in the amount of money spent by each group is not so marked.

- What conclusions might be drawn from the fact that visitors to the UK seem to spend about the same amount of money, in total, as do the many more UK residents who travel abroad (**outbound tourism**)?
- The period of three months ending September 1995 includes the traditional summer-holiday period, yet the figures show that during the next three months to December 1995, even more visits were made abroad. How would you account for this significant increase?
- Obtain the latest figures available from the Office for National Statistics, and construct a line graph similar to the one shown in Figure 1.3 to give an overall impression of the travel and tourism industry today.

Figure 1.5 shows some figures for the distribution of tourism in 1994 to the eleven tourist boards of England and the national tourist boards of Scotland, Wales and Northern Ireland. These figures clearly demonstrate the continued popularity of UK tourism by British residents, as well as the particular destinations favoured by overseas visitors to the UK (**inbound tourism**).

OVERSEAS RESIDENTS' VISITS TO UK
SEASONALLY ADJUSTED

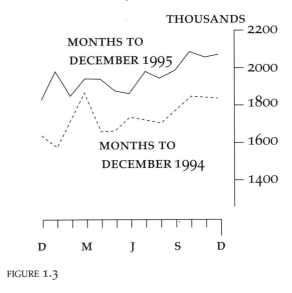

FIGURE 1.3

- Study Figure 1.5. The data presented here is 'raw'. Which other data would be useful when considering the relative distribution of visitors to various parts of the UK?
- Take the total spend for London from Figure 1.5. How would we explain the great difference between what UK residents spend and that amount spent by overseas visitors?

However, both these destinations are seeing changes in levels of popularity in 1996 (though the statistics are not yet available to prove it). In France, there is concern about the relative value of the franc against the pound; and Spain is seeking to improve the image of some of its Costas – so popular with British tourists since the 1950s – both by replacing some of the older hotels and by providing more 'up-market' facilities.

Statistics are also produced to show how people spend their leisure time. Again, such data is very useful to anyone thinking of setting up a business which will be dependent on leisure or tourist customers.

Refer now to the statistics for UK visits abroad in Figure 1.6. Over 70% of all visits made overseas in 1994 were to European Union (EU) countries, with France being the most popular, followed closely by Spain.

FIGURE 1.4 *A summary of statistics for travel and tourism to and from the UK for last 6 months of 1995.*

	Overseas residents' visits to the UK		UK residents' visits abroad	
	Visits (1000s)	**Spending** (£m)	**Visits** (1000s)	**Spending** (£m)
		Seasonally adjusted		
1995				
Jul	1,980	975	3,460	1,285
Aug	1,950	965	3,330	1,225
Sep	1,990	955	3,390	1,320
Oct	2,090	995	3,550	1,300
Nov	2,060	1,005	3,500	1,335
Dec	2,070	1,075	4,220	1,410
Three months ending				
1995 Sep	5,920	2,895	10,180	3,830
1995 Dec	6,220	3,075	11,270	4,045

SOURCE: *Office for National Statistics, 1996.*

FIGURE 1.5 *Distribution of tourism, 1994.*

Millions	UK residents		Overseas visitors	
	Trips	Spending	Trips	Spending
Cumbria	2.9	£425	.30	£53
Northumbria	3.1	£355	.44	£131
North West	8.6	£1,090	1.12	£395
Yorkshire & Humberside	9.3	£1,110	.91	£220
Heart of England	9.9	£1,050	1.34	£378
East Midlands	7.6	£835	.68	£188
East Anglia	10.2	£1,175	1.32	£390
London	8.6	£1.105	11.46	£5,281
West Country	15.1	£2,455	1.46	£399
Southern	10.6	£1,145	1.83	£590
South East	7.9	£900	2.03	£639
England	90.2	£11,650	18.07	£8,671
N. Ireland	1.2	£180	.10	£54
Scotland	8.5	£1,310	1.77	£768
Wales	9.8	£1,075	.69	£190
UK*	109.8	£14,495	21.03	£9,919

*UK includes Channel Islands and the Isle of Man.

SOURCE: *British Tourist Authority/English Tourist Board, 1995.*

FIGURE 1.6 *UK residents' visits abroad, 1992–94.*

	1992	1993	1994	1994 (percentage)
USA	2,450	2,660	2,509	6.3
Canada	363	390	461	1.2
NORTH AMERICA	2,813	3,050	2,970	7.4
Belgium	928	1,012	964	2.4
Luxembourg	29	45	44	0.1
France	7,887	7,816	9,009	22.6
Germany	1,777	1,824	1,898	4.8
Italy	1,223	1,214	1,540	3.9
Netherlands	1,364	1,309	1,414	3.5
Denmark	184	209	229	0.6
Greece	1,908	2,009	2,178	5.5
Spain	5,675	6,441	7,705	19.3
Portugal	1,232	1,095	1,188	3.0
Irish Republic	2,134	2,225	2,491	6.2
EUROPEAN COMMUNITY	24,341	25,199	28,661	71.8
Turkey	329	659	721	1.8
Yugoslavia	22	27	40	0.1
Austria	638	664	590	1.5
Switzerland	629	554	575	1.4
Norway	158	181	183	0.5
Sweden	185	166	192	0.5
Finland	50	64	77	0.2
Iceland	21	21	24	0.1
Gibraltar	31	40	29	0.1
Malta	338	400	468	1.2
Cyprus	934	789	977	2.4
NON-EC WESTERN EUROPE	3,334	3,564	3,875	9.7
Middle East	272	298	356	0.9
North Africa	392	455	511	1.3
South Africa	121	138	134	0.3
Rest of Africa	289	318	381	1.0
Eastern Europe	599	761	726	1.8
Japan	66	69	80	0.2
Australia	256	225	282	0.7
New Zealand	55	68	72	0.2
Commonwealth Caribbean	321	396	415	1.0
Latin America	102	140	156	0.4
Rest of World	874	1,053	1,279	3.2
OTHER COUNTRIES	3,347	3,922	4,391	11.0
TOTAL WORLD	33,836	35,735	39,897	100.0

SOURCE: *Travel Trends, Crown Copyright 1995.*

7

THE STRUCTURE OF THE LEISURE AND TOURISM INDUSTRIES

TASK 4

- Can you suggest what the effects might be for British holiday-makers if France, Spain and other popular venues continue with policies which might reduce their levels of popularity or change the emphasis they place on tourism?
- Produce horizontal bar graphs to show the figures presented in Figure 1.6.

The tables of statistics on the previous page give you some idea of the enormous diversity inherent in the leisure and tourism industries. Many other forms of data collection are also regularly made, and you might wish to send off for more details – see the 'Useful addresses' section at the end of this volume.

As pointed out earlier in this section, the UK leisure and tourism industry, which you have just studied in more detail using various statistical information, is arranged in three main sectors. We now look at each of these sectors in turn.

Key Skills Hint: Application of Number

Collecting data from people – interviews and questionnaires

Two data-collection techniques useful when conducting surveys with people are interviews (face-to-face questioning) and questionnaires (not conducted face-to-face but instead, for example, by post or on the telephone). Some simple guidelines to help you carry out these two techniques are as follows:

Interviews

- Decide on the information you require, and design questions that focus on this information
- Decide on a logical order to your questions
- Don't forget an introductory explanation and a concluding 'Thank you'
- Guard against stereotyping the interviewee according to age or gender or prejudging the answer you will receive by the wording of your question: 'As a woman, I'm sure you will value . . .'
- Don't ask questions on topics of which the interviewee has no knowledge
- When designing questions, think about how you will record the answers – on paper? By tape? – and then collate and analyse them

Questionnaires

- Ensure that the wording of questions is brief and easy to understand – avoid jargon and technical terms where possible
- Give clear guidelines as to how you wish each question to be answered – e.g. 'Please tick ONE box in each row . . .'
- Limit the number of questions you ask, and leave enough space for the respondent to answer
- Use a variety of answering styles to maintain interest – e.g. tick boxes, bipolar questions, yes/no answers, unstructured questions
- Avoid personal questions where possible: respondents may be unwilling to give details such as address or age. If such questions *are* necessary to your survey, place them at the end of your questionnaire!
- Decide on the use of open (unstructured) and closed (structured) questions. Open questions allow respondents to give their full opinions, but can be complex to process. Closed questions permit only a narrow set of answers, but are easier to collate
- Trial your questionnaire before final issue with a small sample of people: this will act as a check that the questionnaire will perform correctly

TASK 5

- Suppose that you are devising a part of the leisure strategy for your local council. How would you translate the national figures shown in Figure 1.7 to your local situation? What recommendations would you wish to make to councillors about local provision? What conclusions can you draw from those forms of provision listed in Figure 1.7 which shows significant differences by gender?

- Carry out a similar survey and compare your own results to those shown in Figure 1.7. You will need a reasonable sample of the local population of both genders aged 16 or over which has been participating in each activity in the three months prior to the interview

FIGURE 1.7 *Participation in leisure activities away from home in the UK, 1994–95.*

	Percentages		
	Males	**Females**	**All persons**
Visit a public house	70	68	64
Meal in a restaurant (not fast food)	60	64	62
Drive for pleasure	47	47	47
Meal in a fast-food restaurant	45	40	42
Library	36	43	40
Cinema	35	32	34
Short break holiday	32	28	30
Disco or night club	29	22	25
Historic building	27	24	25
Spectator sports event	31	13	22
Theatre	19	22	21

SOURCE: *The Henley Centre,*
Social Trends, *Crown Copyright, 1996.*

The public sector

Clearly, organisations in the public sector are operated by national or local authorities and are most likely to be financed out of public funds. These funds are derived from the taxes people pay. Since the early 1990s, government responsibility has been vested with the Department of National Heritage (DNH) which oversees all the activities of national significance for leisure and tourism. Within the DNH, there are five main Directorates, each employing large numbers of civil servants who administrate the huge sums of public money involved. The five Directorates are:

1 the Heritage and Tourism Group
2 the Arts and Lottery Group
3 the Broadcasting, Film and Sport Group
4 Libraries, Galleries and Museums Group
5 the Resources and Services Group.

These Directorates involve many of the groups in which you have a direct interest, and in addition, there are a number of public bodies which act within the remit of the DNH but are run separately from it – i.e. the so-called 'quangos' (quasi-autonomous non-governmental organisations): you will have heard of the Sports Council, English Heritage and the British Film Institute, amongst others.

- Contact one of the quangos listed above, or contact the Department of National Heritage to see if you can discover others. Seek advice about their work, their spheres of influence and how they operate. The Sports Council, for example, devolves responsibility down to the local level, and you may well find that your school or college falls within the area of your local Sports Council. Try then to concentrate your interest on a particular topic. For example, you might wish to investigate the role of the local Sports Council in seeking funds from the National Lottery for local sports and recreational activities. Indeed, your group might wish to instigate an application to the National Lottery for a particular project linked to a local need. Here, you will certainly require the cooperation of your local Sports Council, and your town hall or civic centre will put you in touch with its chairperson
- Another option for your investigation might be to try to discover a project which falls within the tourism or leisure context and which has come before your local council. One example might be an application for consent for floodlighting and an artificial astroturf pitch at a football ground. See if you can pick out the arguments which were made both for and against the proposals. Who won? Who lost? To what extent did local opinion really count? Would the project have assisted recreational activity? It is recommended that you seek the advice of the relevant Officers of the Council, perhaps the Planning Officer or the Leisure and Recreation Officer. Officers will have a much clearer and more detailed overview of the local situation than elected representatives will have
- Write up your investigations in the form of a report about provision in your area. Aim not only to describe the products and services available to the people, but also to give a much better idea, perhaps to a visitor, of just what your area can offer. Illustrate your report in suitable ways with maps, photographs or drawings, and imaginative, easy-to-read text. Also include in your report any information which you have been able to discover about the involvement of other contractors in the running of a facility, or in any aspects of dual use or joint provision which exist

The private sector

Establishments in the private sector are usually owned by an individual or small group of people who want to put their available funds into a project which particularly interests them and which, if run properly, will secure for them some financial profit. Sometimes, the owner(s) will 'float' their company on the stock market, thus giving other individuals the chance to own a share in the organisation and to derive some profit from their investment.

There are a large number of ways in which private facilities are made available for public use. These facilities might include:

- theatres, cinemas, bingo halls, opera houses, discos, nightclubs
- pubs, restaurants, wine bars, cafés, hotels, guesthouses
- leisure centres, health suites, fitness studios, golf courses
- bus and train companies, airlines
- travel agencies, tour operators, theme parks

In fact, there are almost limitless possibilities in the private sector. However, you should understand that here also, it is the management of the operation which really counts and upon which, ultimately, success is measured. A private-sector organisation will usually be run by paid staff who are overseen by a board of directors. Responsible for hiring and firing staff, the board will also want to keep a close eye on the financial situation.

By way of contrast, what do you suppose a small guesthouse has to do in order to compete in the open market, and so derive for its owner as high a return on investment as possible (see Task 7)?

The voluntary sector

This sector of leisure and tourism could well involve you as a voluntary worker in a scheme to help raise the profile of a particular project and so allow it to become more widely known, appreciated and used. The voluntary sector is huge and could involve people from all walks of life who simply want to offer their time and expertise for the common good. Such groups also have to be organised and managed equally as effectively as in the public or private sectors. Usually, paid staff are employed to run the facility and to be responsible to a further group of people, who are also volunteers and who have an interest in the facility and want it to be successful, called a board or management committee.

You will again need to refer to your lists of local facilities. Try to determine which of these facilities are mostly run by volunteers. Here are some which you might have on your lists:

- youth organisations such as Scouts, youth clubs, horse-riding clubs
- church groups, play groups, minority clubs, community-action groups
- environment-aware groups, conservation societies, bird-watching clubs, ramblers groups

There are literally thousands of such organisations, and you will certainly find some in your area.

One of the best-known activities of voluntary groups is concerned with maintaining for the National Heritage some of the old steam railways. It really is amazing how many people are keen to ride on an old steam train which huffs and puffs through some of the country's most outstanding scenery! These railways are often the result of endless hours of painstaking work by an army of enthusiasts who lovingly polish and paint, restore and renovate, these huge machines (see Task 8).

TASK 7

Imagine that you are assisting the owner of a six-bedroomed guesthouse in a British seaside resort. He has been trading for a number of years, but he is finding that profits are slipping, expenses are increasing and urgent action is therefore required. What do you do? Here are some facts to help your thinking:

- The name of the guesthouse is 'Sea Breeze'. The proprietor is Mr T. Regan, who has owned the property for the past eight years
- Mr Regan purchased the property when prices were at their height, and his mortgage repayments are therefore high – around £1,100 a month. Furthermore, gas, electricity and water rates have increased, and business rates (£1,160 a year) and council tax have also gone up
- Mr Regan needs to redecorate the rooms, and has decided to use top-quality materials. He also has to replace some furniture. Guests want extra services these days, such as satellite TV and tea-making materials, and most expect 'en-suite' facilities too. Mr Regan uses welcoming colour schemes, and does his best to create a

'cosy atmosphere' which will cause his guests to come again to stay. He is not a 'take it or leave it' proprietor. In fact, he is a DIY enthusiast

- As part of his quality service, Mr Regan offers a full English Breakfast, a choice of four cereals, fruit or juice, at least six cooked items on the plate, and no limits on tea, coffee, toast, butter and marmalade
- There is a car-parking problem outside the property, and the local council is planning double yellow lines in the near future
- The local Tourist Board offers a room-finding service to its visitors, for which the charges have increased this year. The Board charges customers 10% of the total bill for nights booked plus an administration fee of £1 per head. 'Sea Breeze' displays a sign to say 'Tourist Board Approved' (see Figure 1.8), but this also has to be paid for, and as Mr Regan says, it tells nothing of the quality of service he offers
- The Tourist Board also advertises his guesthouse in the town's brochure, available to all visitors, but this advertisement alone cost him £700 this year. The Yellow Pages advert is even more costly
- The museum in the town has just decided to create a 'moving image' display to better illustrate more of its extensive collection; and the pier authorities are also intending to add more attractions for the next season. Mr Regan is very knowledgeable about the area, and regularly helps his guests to plan their itineraries for the days they are out

So, what would you do to assist Mr Regan in his planning for the next season? How can he increase the number of bed-nights he needs to raise his income and so go into greater profit? How can he keep track of his visitors, and by so doing, check on the effectiveness of his advertising? How does he meet the criteria of the local Tourist Board in running his guesthouse? Think through some of these and other issues, and draw up a list of points which Mr Regan would raise at a meeting, to be held next week between local proprietors, the Tourist Board and council officials, which has been called to seek to address the concern of the industry about next seasons' operations.

FIGURE 1.8 *The 'Sea Breeze' guesthouse – typical of the thousands found all over the UK.*

T A S K   8

The Bluebell Railway in Sussex is one of the UK's foremost preservation societies, operating a fleet of the old steam locomotives. Around 20 people, mostly volunteers, are daily needed to be drivers, firemen, guards, signalmen, station staff, carriage cleaners, booking clerks, and shop and catering staff. And this does not include further people who work behind the scenes to restore and maintain the trains. Here are some headings of leaflets which the Bluebell Railway uses to attract customers to come and ride the trains and to use its services:

- 'Learn to drive and fire a steam locomotive – foot plate days and ways for the real enthusiast!'
- 'Pullman services on the Golden Arrow – enjoy five-star catering as you ride the train through breathtaking scenery!' (see Figure 1.9)
- 'Children's fun weekends aboard the Bluebell – see the brake van, pull the signal levers, operate the whistle!'

Select one of the above, or devise a suitable title of your own. Now design a small publicity pamphlet to sell your ideas to a target market. For example, if you were riding the Pullman Service, what sort of catering and entertainment could be provided; when would you offer really special trips; how much would you charge; where would you advertise; and how would you create (or recreate) the superb atmosphere to make a memorable occasion out of the experience?

FIGURE 1.9 *The Golden Arrow train at Sheffield Park Station on the Bluebell Railway. Its famous restaurant car is a sell-out.*

SOURCE: *Bluebell Railway Operating Ltd, Sheffield Park Station, East Sussex.*

Your local tourist-information office will help you to get in touch with similar facilities to the Bluebell Railway mentioned in the task above. Or you might choose a local church or cathedral, a canal network, a sailing-ship museum, a wildlife centre, a farm offering visits to the public, or a stately home and garden. There are numerous possibilities for places where volunteers are working and organising, fundraising, managing or pressuring for recognition of the projects they support. You can assist them, join their committees, offer your services, devise new plans and, put more simply, get involved in the action!

The Products and Services of the Leisure and Tourism Industries

Key Aims

Working through this section, you will:

- develop an understanding of the major steps through which, historically, the leisure and tourism industries have passed
- understand the products and services of the leisure and tourism industries
- investigate, in the light of case-study material, the provision of facilities in leisure and tourism in your local area

The leisure and tourism industries, like all industries, operate as an **open system** (see Figure 2.1). The organisations and companies involved want to sell or offer you something – a holiday, an admission, an hour of swimming, climbing boots, a tennis racket etc. These are the *inputs.* At the travel agency or the reception desk or the check-in counter, experts then advise you as to the best ways in which to proceed. You might pick up leaflets or other promotional materials. These are the *throughputs.* You then leave the office, having been served properly and efficiently, feeling satisfied with the treatment and advice you have received, or with the goods you have purchased. You have now benefited in some way from the *output* of the system; i.e. its **products and services** have now been made available to you. The system is completed when a proportion of the output is returned, from its profit, to the input by way of offering customers better equipment or more reliable information or better holidays. This is a chance for the industry to invest in itself and so to improve the standards of service given. It also enables firms to carry out **market**

research to ensure that it is selling the right product at the right price. Customers are more likely to return to the industry when they have received good service and have enjoyed the products; and they will rightly complain if they have not. So long as the service they received over the counter was matched by the efficiency of the booking itself – i.e. flights on time, the hotel room clean and comfortable, adequate meals served by pleasant waiting staff, and so on – the customers will be satisfied.

Obviously, the products and services of any organisation serve to determine precisely what it can 'sell' to its customers, but a *quality* service also has to be given. Luckily, there is a great emphasis these days on TQM – **Total Quality Management** – especially in the leisure and tourism industry, and this indeed is the key requirement of successful operations. Customers rightly expect to be served properly, to follow their pastime in a safe and healthy environment, to enjoy really excellent facilities, and to have easy access to museums, castles and other aspects of the national heritage.

T A S K   9

Using Figure 2.1 and the other details given above, create a comprehensive systems diagram for a particular leisure and tourism facility known to you. Does the system appear to work? Identify any possible weaknesses and suggest any changes. Ideally, discuss your findings with the facility concerned, and again modify your diagram as a result of any new ideas that arise. Compare your completed chart with those found in the Beaulieu case study later in this section.

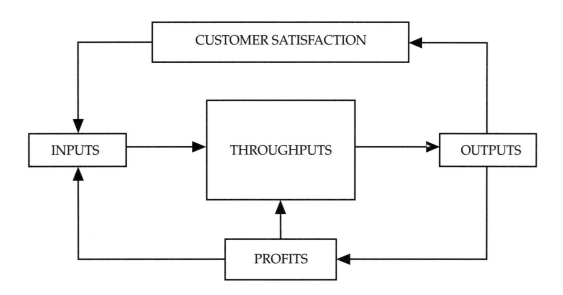

FIGURE 2.1 *A simplified industrial systems diagram.*

TRAVEL IN TIME — THE HISTORICAL DEVELOPMENT OF TRAVEL, TOURISM, LEISURE AND RECREATIONAL ACTIVITY

THE GROWTH OF THOMAS COOK AND P&O

Name any high-street travel operator! An immediate straw poll is likely to identify a list of the more popular: Lunn Poly, Going Places, Thomas Cook (see Figure 2.2) – but there are many others. One of the best-established UK firms is Thomas Cook, a travel company which was formed in the second half of the nineteenth century and which now offers a comprehensive travel service to over 8 million people every year.

Name a major shipping company which operates from British ports! Again, there are many, but one which is sure to feature on a list is the Peninsula and Oriental Steamship Navigation Company, i.e. P&O. This company too is long established, having withstood takeovers and name changes. P&O carries large numbers of passengers each year on its ferries and liners, not to mention the huge quantities of cargo carried by its container ships.

Today, Thomas Cook is owned by a German bank, while the P&O Group continues its tradition as a company which, according to Lord Sterling, P&O's Chairman, 'is only as good as the people who work in it'. Both firms offer high standards of service and levels of expertise, and are widely considered to be world leaders in the industry.

Consider now how these two companies might have developed into the giants they are today. Below appear a number of key facts which will focus your thinking:

- Thomas Cook, aged 32, was Secretary of the Leicester Temperance Society. The arrival of the Midland Railway in 1841 caused him to wonder if this was not the

FIGURE 2.2 *Some well-known high-street travel agents – their shop fronts are made more attractive to customers by special offers and deals.*

way he could carry his members to the more beautiful parts of the country in an atmosphere free of drink and the effects of smoking

- 1837 was the founding year of P&O, a time when the 'dark satanic mills' of the Industrial Revolution began to overwhelm the foreshores of great river estuaries such as the Thames and the Clyde, replacing wooden vessels with iron ships, and sails with steam boilers
- Arthur Anderson and Brodie McGhie Willcox were the founders of P&O. Their first ship was a 206-ton, 60-horsepower paddle steamer (with sails!) which ran their 'Peninsular Steam' service to Spain and Portugal
- Soon (1840), P&O acquired larger ships to carry both mail and passengers across the Atlantic – from Liverpool – and to Alexandria in Egypt. The Far East, with its uncharted waters and dangerous pirates, was also home to P&O ships
- The first Thomas Cook leisure trip was to Liverpool in 1845, with an optional excursion by a steamer to Caernarvon in North Wales
- In 1851, the year of the Great Exhibition in Hyde Park, London, Thomas Cook made travel arrangements for 165,000 visitors. By 1861, Thomas Cook was escorting visits for ordinary folk to Paris, and in 1867 a hotel coupon scheme was launched which we would recognise now as an integral part of a 'package holiday'
- In 1869, Thomas Cook escorted his first party of 32 people to Egypt and Palestine, with steamer trips up the Nile. In the same year he attended the opening of the Suez Canal
- When the Suez Canal opened, P&O had to realise that

  the voyage down the Red Sea and across the Indian Ocean was east or south-east and, on the return, the opposite. Both ways, the cabins on the more northerly side were consequently cooler ... and

people aware of their own importance wanted cabins on the cooler side of the ships ...

'Port Out, Starboard Home', they demanded!

- In 1874, Thomas Cook's 'Circular Note' was issued, the first form of traveller's cheque. Easily transferred money values between nations began (but still has not been totally resolved!)
- By 1884, P&O's fleet had grown to 50 ships with an average tonnage of 3,700, and the Suez Canal had been widened and deepened to take these. The advent of the electric telegraph was important at this time: owners could now communicate directly with their ships, telling them to pick up cargo and passengers at will. Paddle steamers were replaced by ships propelled by twin screws, and P&O began to carry large numbers of emigrant passengers to Australia, often 1,100 at a time, via the Cape
- Thomas Cook had offices in many countries by this time, including Australia, India and North America. The first world tour had also taken place (1872). Large numbers of customers visited the Paris Exhibition of 1878: 400,000 tickets were issued by Thomas Cook, and 20,000 clients also purchased sightseeing tours of the city. Cruises on the River Nile were now solely operated by the company
- The turn of the century began an expansion of both companies. Thomas Cook was soon planning motorcar tours and winter-sports itineraries. P&O took over the British India Shipping Line and formed a company with over 200 ships, all carrying freight, mail and passengers. The British Empire was in its heyday, and the Industrial Revolution had produced immense wealth and power for the UK. Workers from the dirty factories and mines had more available cash and wanted to enjoy the fresh air of the seaside
- War was imminent in 1914, and P&O's vessels became armed merchant cruisers and

troopships. Many ships were subsequently lost, but P&O was reformed after the war and began a huge expansion of freight, passenger and emigration journeys to North America, Australia and New Zealand. In the meantime, the Thomas Cook company produced its first air-travel brochure in 1919: 'Aerial travel for business or pleasure'; and in 1920 regular flights to Europe were under way

- Coach and train tours were introduced in the late 1920s and early 1930s. In 1936, 8,000 Canadian ex-servicemen travelled with Cook's to France for the unveiling of the Canadian War Memorial at Vimy Ridge on the Somme battlefields
- In 1929, the P&O liner *Viceroy of India* was introduced into service. This was a 20,000-ton ship with steam turbines driving turbo-electric engines with 17,000 horsepower and a top speed of 19 knots. Cruising was now popular, and more ships such as the *Strathard* and *Strathnaver*, the 'White Sisters', entered the fleet. This was the pinnacle of sea travel
- The 1939–45 War then intervened, and there was terrible loss of tonnage. However, the 1950s, when the British were told that they had 'never had it so good', saw a continuing rise in disposable income, sufficient to allow more and more leisure time, and more and more travel. The popularity of British seaside resorts began to decline in favour of package holidays by air to the Mediterranean, but some of these resorts established themselves as conference and business travel centres – Brighton, for example, in the 1970s – to compensate
- The 1980s and 1990s have seen a decrease in working hours, there are signs of 'the leisure society' emerging, and more and more inventive ways are being found to use up spare time for leisure and recreation, travel and tourism. P&O launched its latest cruise liner, the *Oriana*, a 67,000-ton giant of the seas, in 1995, once again reinforcing the company's belief in the popularity of cruises and commitment to superb levels of comfort and service. Furthermore,

there are now over 1,300 Thomas Cook travel offices in over 100 countries

Through these milestones in the development of the two companies, you will be able to pick out some of the key steps which have influenced the growth of the leisure and tourism industries.

PRODUCTS AND SERVICES

The next two case studies are designed to focus your thinking about the products and services of the leisure and tourism industries. From your work on the *structure* of the leisure and tourism industries, you will already have discovered that, within each industry, certain organisations and facilities can be identified. A summary of these are:

Leisure and recreation

- Arts and entertainment facilities such as galleries, cinemas, theatres, opera houses, bingo halls, antiques and craft fairs, and many others
- Sports and physical-activity facilities such as leisure centres, swimming halls, bowling clubs, squash and badminton clubs, fitness suites, and so on
- Outdoor activity facilities such as climbing and fell-walking clubs, watersports centres, soccer clubs, national parks, garden centres, allotment gardens, shopping malls and hypermarkets, and many others
- Heritage facilities such as museums, castles, sites of special scientific interest, properties of the National Trust, and hundreds of others
- Play facilities such as children's playgrounds, fun fairs, tennis clubs, amusement arcades and lots more
- Catering and accommodation facilities usually associated with some of the above, for example at sports clubs or in museums, and the provision of meeting and conference rooms, youth hostels, and many more examples

THE PRODUCTS AND SERVICES OF THE LEISURE AND TOURISM INDUSTRIES

TASK 10

You should work in two subgroups, one covering leisure and recreation, the other travel and tourism. Refer also to Section 1, Task 1 and Task 17 later in this booklet. In your group, investigate further some of the factors which have led to the popularity of leisure or tourism both in your area and nationally. Consider such factors as: the increase in leisure time, the growth of disposable income, the availability of transport offering increased access (e.g. Eurostar – see Figure 2.3), changing individual needs, and the growth of inbound tourism. Select one particular aspect of present-day leisure and tourism, and using access to CD-ROM if available, trace its development over time, explaining its national availability and the reasons for its distribution. Share the results of your groups' investigations with the other group, and try to explain common features and results. Make notes from the other group's research to include in your final report.

FIGURE 2.3 *Eurostar trains at Waterloo Station, London – like lions in a cage! From London to Paris, city centre to city centre, they are often as fast as a plane journey.*

Travel and tourism

- Travel-service organisations such as travel agencies, bus and coach operators, business-travel operators, tour organisers, package-tour operators, railway-station booking offices, ferry-service offices, airline offices, car-hire firms, and many others
- Tourism facilities such as national tourist boards, tourist-information offices, guided tours, currency-exchange offices, 'honey pot' tourist attractions such as Dover

Castle or the National Gallery, hotels and guesthouses offering accommodation and catering, restaurants, public houses, and many, many more

Identify a UK example for each of the categories listed above for leisure and recreation and travel and tourism facilities. For each example:

- describe the products and services it offers
- explain its location or distribution – this may be due to natural features or accessibility to customers, for example

CASE STUDY: THE NATIONAL MOTOR MUSEUM, BEAULIEU, HAMPSHIRE

Almost everyone has heard of Beaulieu! This is because since 1951, Lord Montagu of Beaulieu has established a reputation from converting his estate, which has been in his family since the mid-sixteenth century, into a tourist **honey pot** which is visited by more than half a million people every year, and which has made a significant impact on the UK's national heritage. The National Motor Museum is part of this honey pot, but within the 2,800 hectares of the estate, tourists are also welcomed at the villages of Beaulieu and Buckler's Hard, the foreshore of the Beaulieu River, the Beaulieu Palace and Abbey, and the 40-bed residential centre of the Countryside Education Trust for organised studies, called the Out of Town Centre, on the home farm of the estate.

To give you an impression of the complexity of running such a large facility, refer to the systems diagrams for the organisation and management of the Beaulieu estate shown in Figures 2.5 and 2.6. The Beaulieu organisation is unique in the way in which its large staff is employed and deployed. Lord Montagu and his senior managers view every employee as part of the Montagu family and they are treated and trained as such. Everyone knows their role as being part of the overall operation. The key to success of the venture is clear: visitors *are* the business. This stress on personal responsibility has its effects right through the operation, and visitors are made to feel really welcome from the outset. This is an enviable record at a place which welcomes so many people every year!

FIGURE 2.4 *The Beaulieu logo at the entrance to the National Motor Museum.*

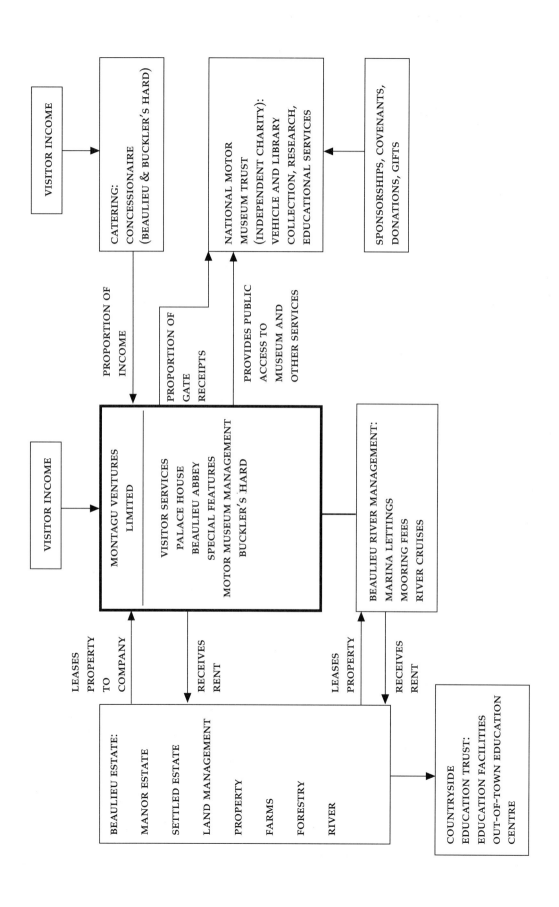

FIGURE 2.5 *The organisation and management of the Beaulieu estate.*
SOURCE: *Montagu Ventures Ltd.*

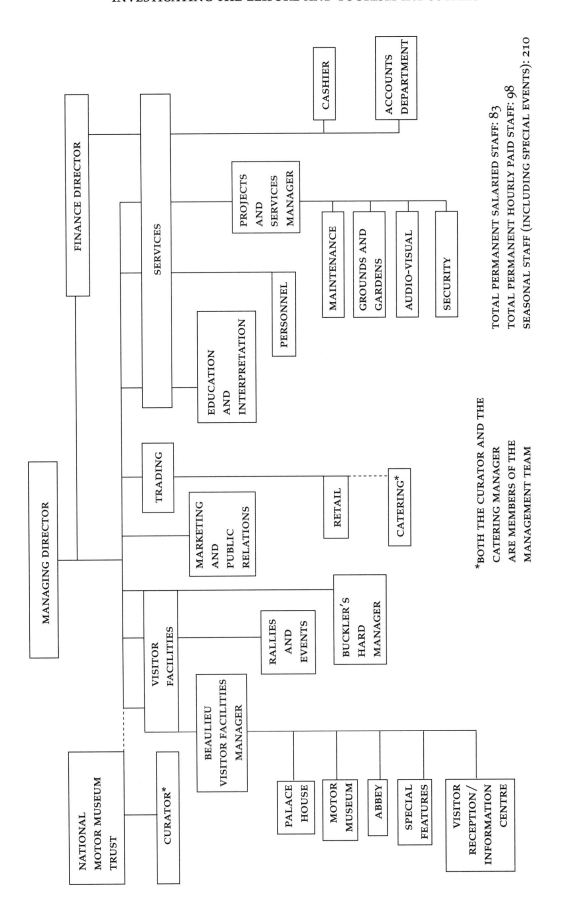

FIGURE 2.6 *The Montagu Ventures management structure.*
SOURCE: *Montagu Ventures Ltd.*

TOTAL PERMANENT SALARIED STAFF: 83
TOTAL PERMANENT HOURLY PAID STAFF: 98
SEASONAL STAFF (INCLUDING SPECIAL EVENTS): 210

*BOTH THE CURATOR AND THE CATERING MANAGER ARE MEMBERS OF THE MANAGEMENT TEAM

TASK 12

Here is the 'mission statement' of the Beaulieu organisation:

To ensure the continued existence and continual enhancement of the Beaulieu estate as an entity in family ownership, as an area of outstanding natural beauty and an integral part of the New Forest and to make appropriate areas of the estate accessible for public enjoyment.

(a) Determine into which of the three industry sectors this facility falls.

(b) The main aims of the central structure of the organisation (Montagu Ventures Ltd) fall into four main categories:

  1 to provide public access to sites suitable for leisure and recreational activities at Beaulieu and Buckler's Hard, while protecting more sensitive areas of the estate.
  2 to manage leisure facilities at Beaulieu and Buckler's Hard, including Palace House and gardens, Beaulieu Abbey, the National Motor Museum and, at Buckler's Hard, the village, historic cottages and Maritime Museum.
  3 to market these facilities . . .
  4 to apply income from leisure activities . . .

Complete aims 3 and 4 above to give an overall perspective of the management functions of the Beaulieu organisation. Your thinking for these aims is likely to cover such aspects as the avoidance of overcrowding, the spoiling of the physical environment, the need to improve visitor facilities, the conservation of buildings and landscapes, and other matters which need to be addressed and borne in mind by the authorities at the estate.

(c) Study the two flow charts, Figures 2.5 and 2.6. Try to apply the systems approach used earlier in this section. Create an 'overlay' of inputs, throughputs and outputs, perhaps colour-coding the various parts.

(d) The management structure for Montagu Ventures Ltd gives you a clear idea of several occupations within the organisation. Make an attempt to list these, and try to discover, in consultation with your careers staff, which qualifiations are likely to be needed for the skills basis of each management tier.

(e) List the products and services offered at Beaulieu. Compare these with the products and services available in a travel-industry facility that you have researched.

The Beaulieu Motor Museum is one of the top 'living history' museums for the motor industry in the UK. The collection is housed in modern surroundings, and there are over 200 vehicles (see Figure 2.7) supported by a variety of thematic displays and audio-visual presentations which are often sponsored by the various suppliers to the motor trade. There is also a fascinating ride-through display which traces the significant advances made during the history of the motor vehicle.

Upon entering the museum complex, visitors purchase tickets (see Figure 2.8) which allow them the flexibility both to wander through the motor museum and to view and take advantage of various other attractions such as the 'Driving Experience' simulator, the veteran bus rides or the monorail which takes visitors around the grounds of the Palace. They can also visit the Palace itself and enjoy the treasures which it contains. There is a free-flow arrangement so that

FIGURE 2.7 *Part of the collection of Rolls-Royce cars at the Beaulieu Motor Museum.*

visitors, once admitted, can wander around at will, enabling them to create an excursion suited to their own particular needs.

CASE STUDY: PLAY SCHEMES — THE WORLD OF CHILDREN'S FANTASY

One way in which we might consider the products and services of the leisure and recreation industry is to look more closely at one of the faster-developing sectors, namely how younger children use their leisure time. You might well find that playgrounds and play schemes are available near you, and this case study, which uses the experiences of one of the world's largest suppliers of playground equipment, Kompan A/S, a Danish company, investigates the philosophy of play and how this is met in the local area. You are to carry out your own research at a local playground facility, and to confirm (or otherwise) the idea that the constructive use of leisure time in later life very much depends on how varied and adventurous play has been in the formative years.

FIGURE 2.8 *Customers at Beaulieu purchase their tickets in the modern arrival hall and shopping centre.*
SOURCE: *National Motor Museum, Beaulieu.*

The joy of playing

The key influences on a child's ability to develop and survive come from their direct life experiences. Through play, children experiment with themselves and their surroundings, and even casual observation will confirm that children use every opportunity to touch, smell, look, taste, listen and feel. In all circumstances, however, there must be concern for safety and health issues, and stringent precautions are necessary to ensure that official guidelines are met.

Children play for the sake of playing. They do not choose a particular activity for a specific purpose; they simply choose to do things which will improve their skills and develop their interests to suit the particular moment. The argument could be made, therefore, that the greater the number of play opportunities which exist in a playground, the greater the chances for different sensory experiences, opportunities for physical activities and role play, social interaction, creativity and a heightening of the senses of security and achievement. How can these latter senses be captured in a playground?

The children shown in Figure 2.9 are clearly totally immersed in their scrambler trip! Careful observation of the photo shows that:

- the equipment is strong and sturdy
- the materials used are free of sharp edges
- the bolts and fittings are protected against corrosion: they are covered with a rounded, self-locking protective cap made from shock-resistant nylon
- through-fittings are locked tight upon manufacture and do not require servicing

Further observation of Figure 2.9 might lead you to consider other factors concerning safety. The youngster in the pillion seat could get his left foot caught in the spring. The driver could knock his chin. The rocking and rolling could tip both children off the bike. However, all of these possibilities have been considered by the designers. The spring has a very limited travel, specially designed not to trap hands and feet, a bump could happen in any circumstance, and the fall is just part of the fun of it all: children cannot be wrapped in cotton wool!

The equipment shown in Figure 2.10 takes further the idea of **junk playgrounds** or 'adventure playgrounds', which in fact were started in Denmark in the mid-1940s. Try to observe from this figure the number of activities which could take place.

You should be aware of an area of concern about playground safety. The Consumer Safety Unit at the Department of Trade and Industry carries out something called the Leisure Accident Surveillance System (LASS). This project investigates the nature of accidents at playgrounds, and compares provision in the UK with that in other countries also in the European Union. You might try to determine how many (if any) accidents have occurred at playgrounds in your area, and your local hospital authority might assist you in this. It is currently the case that huge amounts of public money are used in providing rubberised surfaces in playgrounds in the UK, whereas other European countries prefer sandy or bark-filled

FIGURE 2.9 *The Kompan Crazy Scrambler.*
SOURCE: *Kompan A/S.*

FIGURE 2.10 *The Kompan Big Tower.*
SOURCE: *Kompan A/S.*

surface areas on which to situate their playground equipment. Usually, it is found that where behaviour at the playground is natural and unenforced, the resulting accident rate – from whichever source – is reduced.

Your studies may provide you with interesting evidence about the nature of play at your local playground.

TASK 13

Now it's time for you to look at the play provision of your local area. You might well find that there is a playground in your local town; in any case, the leisure and recreation department of your local authority should be able to assist you in finding the nearest multi-purpose playground available for you to study, and to show you the official documents which control its construction and use. The task is to assess the effectiveness of the provision you find, and to measure it against certain criteria:

- Ascertain when the playground is most frequently used. Carry out an analysis over time on the age range of users and the frequency of use
- Interview parents/guardians. Ascertain their views on play, and find out why they frequent this particular playground

- From interviews, find out how far people are prepared to travel to a proper playground
- Determine the effectiveness of the equipment, especially in terms of its safety, but do look also for examples of imaginative/creative usage
- Interview some of the children. Determine why and how they use the playground. Observe their play, and determine the effectiveness of the equipment
- Report on your findings, perhaps as part of an in-depth investigation of leisure services in your locality. Such a report could be supported by appropriate audio-visual presentations, and can conclude with any recommendations you might have for the attention of the local authority, parents, planners or even children who might not be aware of the provisions available to them in their locality

3

The Impact of the Leisure and Tourism Industries

··

Key Aims

Working through this section, you will:

- investigate some of the economic, social and environmental impacts which leisure and tourism activities exert on an area
- look at examples of how the effects of these impacts can be tackled
- consider the role of tourist boards in the context of the impacts of leisure and tourism activities

All industries exert some impact or pressure on the area in which they are found, and leisure and tourism are no exception. These impacts each have their effect at national, regional and local levels. Once again, you will need to refer to the lists you have drawn up of your local leisure and tourism facilities and organisations. First, though, let us consider what we mean by the following three types of impact: economic impact, social impact, environmental impact. Figure 3.1 on page 28 explores the issues concerned.

SUSTAINABLE TOURISM

Some people have claimed that leisure and tourism combined can cause an area to be 'loved to death'. This is a powerful commentary on the state of the industry today. Figure 3.1 only scratches the surface. Perhaps what is needed is a concerted approach by all concerned to try to harmonise the various problems which have arisen and so prevent tourist 'honey pots' from ruining beauty spots, destroying precious landscapes, polluting

FIGURE 3.1 *Positive and negative economic, social and environmental impacts from leisure and tourism.*

Type of impact	Effects on an area
Economic impacts	
Positive aspects	Create jobs and bring added income to an area – the **multiplier effect**; create more trade amongst local suppliers; make an area more wealthy, because people spend what they have earned out of leisure and tourism. There's a 'feel good factor' when an area is prosperous, and further investment is then attracted to support and develop this prosperity.
Negative aspects	Overspecialisation in leisure or tourism causes an imbalance in the local economy; there could be a loss of industry and jobs; there are seldom all-year-round opportunities since work is seasonal.
Social impacts	
Positive aspects	Create jobs; bring the area to the attention of greater numbers of people; satisfy community aspirations; encourage people to work together to provide for visitors; promote local specialities, crafts and customs; encourage earnings in the locality to then be used in refurbishment projects.
Negative aspects	Too many visitors causes tension in the local community; overspecialisation 'poaches' labour from traditional local industry; tourists are exploited by those seeking quick profits; visitors with money are envied by locals; increased crime rates; visitors do not appreciate local customs.
Environmental impacts	
Positive aspects	A greater awareness of environmental issues by organisations means that care, conservation and preservation issues are addressed; treasured buildings are restored; run-down areas are improved; amenities for everyone to enjoy are introduced; visitors and locals are valued for the contributions to the environment they can make, rather than for the opposite destructive effects which usually gain more publicity.
Negative aspects	Too many visitors causes overcrowding; physical wear and tear on resources occurs, footpaths are trampled, animals are aggravated; litter, noise and the pollution of air, water and surrounding landscapes become a problem; traffic congestion and parking problems also occur.

coasts and countryside, and damaging whole communities and their especially distinctive characteristics. How are we to address these issues?

We have already discovered that the leisure and tourism industries are growth areas, and that more and more people are therefore enjoying leisure and tourism – the '**leisure society**'. However, we have also seen that leisure and tourism can bring side-effects which are not always welcome. In trying to face up to these concerns, the term '**sustainable tourism**' has entered the debate. In defining this concept, discussion has centred on a type of tourism and tourism management which maintains the economic, social and environmental integrity and well-being of both the natural environment and the **built environment** as well as the cultural resources of an area, so that these can be fully enjoyed both now and in the future. We have already seen in this volume that the authorities in Beaulieu show a total commitment to the maintenance of the natural and built environment of the Beaulieu estate, and that the income from visitors to this estate is very largely used to guarantee that end. We have also seen how a relatively small organisation

T A S K   1 4

- Select a number of the organisations which you have identified in your local area. Using a similar tabular format to that found in Table 3.1, identify those leisure and tourism facilities and organisations which bring about any of the three types of impact listed. Do you see any solutions to negative impacts? Can any of the problems be solved, in your judgement?
- Study Figures 3.2 and 3.3. Each shows a public place designed to cater for public needs. One is of the brand new multi-purpose Castle Mall in central Norwich, Norfolk, and the other is of the Seaview Café on the north Norfolk coast, near Cromer. Each provides for widely differing needs. What, in your estimation, are the impacts that each has on the environment? How do you suppose each facility is perceived by its users? What steps would you take to equalise the impacts you have identified?

FIGURE 3.3 *The Castle Mall Shopping Centre, Norwich – does all this glitter and glitz demonstrate progress?*

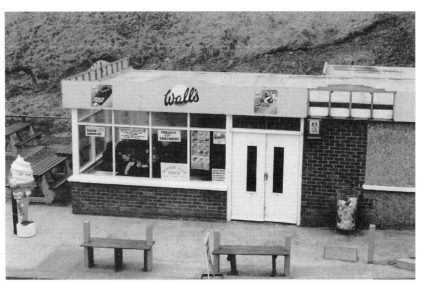

FIGURE 3.2 *The Seaview Café near Cromer, Norfolk – is this a typical eyesore on the environment?*

such as the Bluebell Railway similarly accepts an overall responsibility for maintaining the beauty of the countryside in which it operates.

Leisure and tourism activities involve three matters of concern:

1 the place being visited;
2 the local community;
3 the tourists who wish to visit the area and take part in its events.

Each of these matters needs to be considered in more detail:

1 The *place* being visited has to be treated with respect, its **carrying capacity** observed and overcrowding avoided. Some places are visited by so many people that steps have had to be taken to limit such pressure from visitors. Stonehenge is an example of this. Suggestions were made at one time to build a replica of the great stone circles nearby, but now visitors are instead kept to defined paths and are not allowed to walk amongst the stones, and the car and coach parks have been moved far into the background.

Traffic congestion is another factor at tourist destinations. Increasingly, cars and coaches are kept out of town centres, and 'park and ride' schemes (see Figure 3.4) have been introduced. The Yorkshire Dales and parts of the Lake District have very strict policies regarding car and coach access. Real efforts are being made to **pedestrianise** town and city centres, thus enabling visitors to more fully enjoy what they have come to see.

2 The *local community* is often the first to suffer from a huge influx of tourists or pleasure-seekers. Some of the villages of the Cotswolds and in Devon and Cornwall have suffered particularly badly. Local people expect to be involved in the discussions about the provision of amenities. Naturally, the local community can benefit through an increased number of jobs, and by the fact that visitors will frequent local cafés and restaurants and buy souvenirs in the shops. In other places, however, visitors do not benefit the community. For example, people who can afford holiday homes in, say, rural Wales often bring their provisions with them from their own local supermarkets. Although more jobs may be created in some communities, the fact is that employment is often only seasonal or at weekends, and this too impacts on the area. Where leisure facilities are concerned, it is often a good idea to allow the locals to use them at a reduced cost, thus making the community feel that it owns the facility and is welcomed by it too.

FIGURE 3.4 *A Norwich City Park and Ride bus, helping to keep traffic out of the city centre.*
SOURCE: *Norfolk County Council.*

T A S K   1 5

- Consider one of the leisure or tourism facilities located in your area. You may have noted one which appears to have a greater impact than others. Carry out an Environmental Impact Assessment (EIA) using the matrix shown in Figure 3.5. You may be able to think of additional types of impact besides those given. The use of an EIA is often mandatory when planners are considering a major development since the result of the EIA will enable decision-makers to make a subjective judgement about the significance of each impact. When carrying out your EIA, therefore, you will need to consider critically each type of impact and award a suitable score according to your best judgement and knowl-edge of the locality. You need to consult others, especially neighbours and users of the facility, to assist you in arriving at your conclusions. Here, you are likely to obtain invaluable assistance from the planning officer of your local council. Try to be as impartial as you can. Include extra information on any social and economic impacts you identify

- Use your EIA to make a class presentation, using audio-visual aids such as recordings of interviews, photographs or slides and OHP transparencies. At the conclusion of your presentation, invite a vote to establish whether your EIA is confirmed by the views of others

FIGURE 3.5 *An Environmental Impact Assessment Matrix.*

	Evaluation of impact				
Type of impact	No impact	Minor impact	Moderate impact	Severe impact	Comments
Land use/recreational use					
Ecology					
Surface/ground water					
Air quality					
Noise					
Visual and landscape impact					
Construction impact					
Traffic					
Archaeological impact					
Scores					

3 *Tourists and visitors* need to exercise respect, tolerance and care towards the place they are visiting or using. Sustainable tourism means encouraging people to follow particular codes, and a 'Tourism Charter' is increasingly being used to persuade tourists to act properly and to behave sensibly. Amongst the recommendations of such a Charter are:

- using local shops to purchase food, souvenirs, crafts and products so that earnings stay in the area and do not 'leak' to outside companies or individuals wanting to make quick profits
- understanding that local people have the right to their own lives and privacy, and do not always want noise, aggravation and hassle from careless visitors
- leaving cars and coaches outside the area of interest, and if necessary, transferring to park-and-ride vehicles or proceeding on foot or by bicycle instead. Avoiding peak times also helps a great deal
- learning more about the locality before the visit takes place so as to make it easier to be in contact with the locals, to understand their thoughts and to appreciate their characteristics
- treating the physical environment with respect, staying on marked footpaths, keeping off private property and being fully aware of the often unique wildlife of the area

Leisure and tourism generate large sums of money. Figure 3.6 shows earnings and expenditure at current prices in thousands of pounds (£). The incomes earned are shared by everyone involved in the industry. The figures in the table indicate a negative balance between income from overseas visitors to the UK and expenditure by British tourists travelling overseas. This imbalance has clear consequences for the impacts argument. Should we encourage more tourists? Should we create more leisure and recreational activities and encourage overseas visitors to come and use

them? Certainly, the imbalance needs attention. Maybe we charge too much: many visitors are heard complaining about the cost and standards of our hotels; others say that admission charges are high compared to other countries; and many complain that our infrastructure – such as our roads, railways and bus routes – is clogged up, dirty and expensive. Now that the Channel Tunnel is fully operational, maybe more of our near neighbours will visit us (see also Figure 3.9). Are we geared up for such an eventuality?

THE BRITISH TOURIST AUTHORITY

Any increase in the number of visitors to the UK is a result of the effectiveness of the marketing function, of which you will learn more later in your course. Salespersons in the UK's tourist industry work hard at promoting us abroad. Indeed, there are British Tourist Authority (BTA) offices in 41 countries, 23 of which are open to the public. Between them, they account for 85% of inbound tourism to the UK. Over 2.5 million enquiries a year are handled, including 600,000 at the British Travel Centre in Lower Regent Street, London. Some £35.5 million has been set aside by the Department of National Heritage (DNH) for the activities of the BTA in 1996–97. Overall, therefore, the UK leisure and tourism scene seems well provided for! In almost every village, town and city, and perhaps every rural area in the country, there are signs of leisure and tourism activity. Too much activity, possibly? Maybe it is all a question of emphasis.

FIGURE 3.6 *Earnings and expenditure from travel and tourism, in thousands of pounds.*

Year	Overseas visitors to the UK (income)	UK residents going abroad (expenditure)	Balance
1990	7,748	9,886	−2,138
1991	7,386	9,951	−2,565
1992	7,891	11,243	−3,352
1993	9,354	12,705	−3,351
1994	9,919	14,500	−4,581
1995	11,735	15,460	−3,725

SOURCE: *Office for National Statistics, 1996.*

Every British region is represented by the BTA. There are 11 regional tourist boards in England (see Figure 1.5) as well as separate tourist boards for Wales, Scotland and Northern Ireland. The BTA lists the following strategic objectives as being the responsibilities of each of the regional tourist boards:

- to have a thorough knowledge of tourism within the region, and of the facilities and organisations involved in the tourism industry (see Figure 3.7)
- to advise the national board on the regional aspects of major policy issues, and to supply management information
- to service enquiries attributable to a nationally developed promotion, and to provide relevant literature
- to coordinate regional tourist-information services as part of the national network
- to maintain a close liaison with planning authorities on policies affecting tourism
- to carry out a continuing domestic public-relations campaign with the local authorities, the travel trade and the public within the region, with a view to ensuring that issues are understood and the regional and national objectives known; to create awareness of the need for tourism to be managed for the benefit of residents as well as tourists
- to promote tourism to the region both from other parts of the country and from overseas

(SOURCE: *British Tourist Authority*)

FIGURE 3.7 *An English tourist board exhibition. Here, local attractions can advertise themselves to the travel trade and the public.*

T A S K   1 6

- Consider Figures 3.8 and 3.9. Each shows a popular tourist destination in the UK. The photo of Shaftesbury, in Thomas Hardy's Dorset, shows how effective the complete barring of traffic to the scene has been. A number of the properties shown are B&B guest-houses, and most of the buildings are **listed properties**.

 The photo of Bramber in West Sussex shows a popular country pub and hotel which has links with other similar places in the county; and the Channel Tunnel is just 2 hours away by motorway. This village is bypassed, and there are humps and other **calming measures** to restrict the speed of cars. People can therefore hardly fail to see 'Ye Bramber Castle Hotel'! Draw up lists of features shown in the two photos which clearly indicate the travel and tourism potential of each venue.

 The likely impacts of tourists in each area are in fact quite different. Which do you think are the most likely impacts in each case? What additional steps might be taken to protect the integrity of each area so that everyone benefits?

- Look again at the 'Tourism Charter' recommendations on p. 32. Are you in sympathy with the points made? Make up a 'Tourist's Charter' or a 'Leisure User's Charter' for your town or area which you might hand to visitors, with suitable permission. Monitor the results, and retain your findings

- Interview local people and obtain their views about visitors to their area. Investigate local attitudes, look at employment patterns and try to find out the extent to which leisure/tourism benefits the local community

FIGURE 3.8 *A scene from yesteryear – the old High Street in Shaftesbury, Dorset, completely closed to traffic.*

FIGURE 3.9 *The Castle Hotel, Bramber, West Sussex, a small country hotel in rural beauty, not far from the Channel Tunnel for foreign visitors.*

On the Crest of a Wave? Developing Dover's Leisure and Tourism Industries

....

K e y   A i m s

Working through this section, you will:

- consider, through further case studies, how a British town is building on its strengths and seizing new opportunities to develop its leisure and tourism potential
- investigate some of the issues arising out of the intense competition which exists to succeed in the industry
- tackle an in-depth decision-making task which will help in the revision of all of this Unit's investigations

This final section is a detailed case-study analysis based on the emerging port of Dover. Please also refer to Figure 4.1. A series of tasks completes the study. Three major operators of the leisure and tourism industry in Dover are investigated. They are widely differing organisations, but each, through its operations, involves a common theme: the effects of the Channel Tunnel. It might seem strange to describe Dover as an 'emerging' port. After all, Dover has a very long history as the foremost UK cross-Channel seaport, and as the nearest port to France. However, the Channel Tunnel has caused a fundamental rethink about Dover's role in cross-Channel operations, and it is this rethink that we now investigate.

The three case studies involve the following issues:

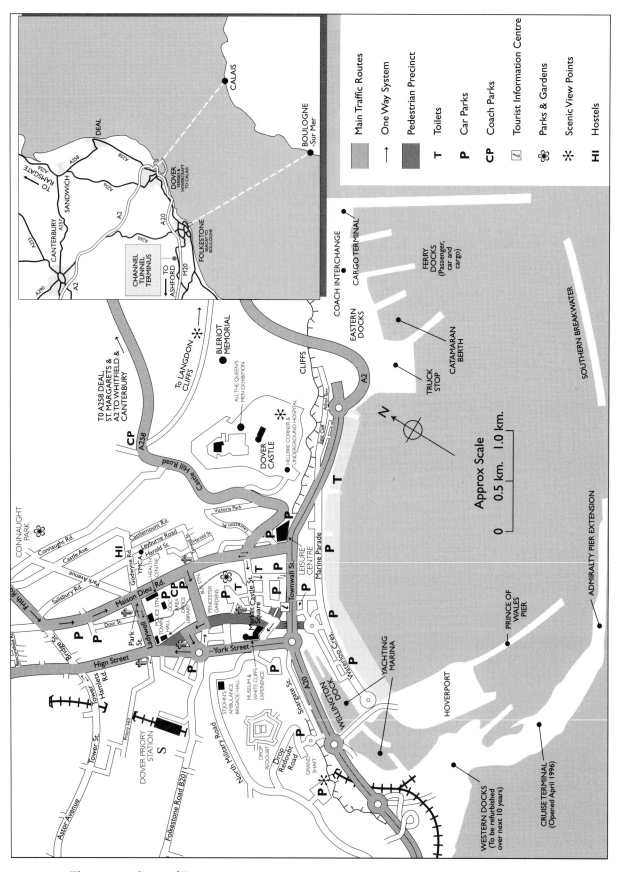

FIGURE 4.1 *The town and port of Dover.* SOURCE: *Adapted from a map produced by the Dover Tourist Information Office.*

1 The P&O European Ferries operations are first considered. With more Britons than ever heading for France in the summer of 1996, and with three other major competitors for their business, surely there has to come a time when rationalisation of the vast carrying capacity of superferries, hovercrafts, catamarans, Eurostar and Le Shuttle will be necessary?

2 Up to 50,000 people a day now cross the English Channel in each direction. The White Cliffs Experience has been designed as one of the attractions in Dover which will try to persuade visitors to stay for a while in the town instead of just passing through it. How will it do that?

3 The Dover Harbour Board operates all movements in and out of the port. Supposing that ferries do have to give way to the Tunnel, where will the Board's revenue then come from? The Board is looking for new ideas, and recently invested £9 million in a brand new terminal – not for cross-Channel ferries but for cruise liners.

CASE STUDY: P&O'S EUROPEAN FERRIES OPERATION

As we have already seen in this volume, P&O has a long and distinguished history as a shipping company. This is especially true of the cross-Channel market, which analysts have recently described as being one of the business phenomena of the 1990s. Few industries would have been able to sustain a potential 50% increase in capacity, as has happened with the opening of the Channel Tunnel, without facing a potentially ruinous reduction in profit margins. While all the carriers operating from Dover – i.e. P&O European Ferries, Stena, Sea France and Eurotunnel – do face some form of rationalisation of service both during 1996 and into the late 1990s, plans are nonetheless in hand to introduce even better, larger and faster ships to the route; and Eurotunnel in turn intends to put on even more, faster trains! Why has there been such an increase in traffic to France? Some would point to the effectiveness of the publicity, others to the attraction of duty-free purchases and cheaper goods on the Continent, and others to the extremely competitive prices being offered, especially in the off-season. There is a **price war** in progress, but this cannot go on indefinitely. Indeed, during the Summer of 1996, the Government permitted the ferry operators to cooperate over future planning issues. This has allowed the operators to take on Eurotunnel with a concerted approach. There is even talk of amalgamations between the operators which will certainly produce keen competition with the Tunnel. It may also have the effect of ending the price war and increasing prices again.

For all the ferry operators, there has been a decline in market share, and whereas the Tunnel during the first full year of its operation, carried only 26% of all tourist vehicles, this figure is predicted to rise to nearer 50% in 1996 and beyond. How does a major ferry operator face the challenge? It can perhaps do two things:

1 keep pressing forwards, hoping that the continued expansion in the market as a whole will sustain it;

2 set out to recapture some of the Tunnel's business by being better at meeting the all-important, customer-related criterion: *quality of service.*

P&O has elected to do both! It intends to set the standard that the Channel Tunnel will have to match, and which its competitors too will have to continue to emulate. As the market leader, P&O has invested millions of pounds both in tonnage and in improving passenger facilities on board. It has introduced a 'Club Class' for travellers, recognising that passengers are increasingly discerning, wanting to be treated as individuals and willing to pay both for privileges and for a quality product. The Club Class allows the holiday-maker, and increasingly the business executive, to relax in luxurious, exclusive surroundings with steward service. The business traveller can use the crossing for catching up on the news, and if they wish, for working at specially appointed work stations with full communications services to hand.

FIGURE 4.2 *One of P&O's flagship ferries, the Pride of Calais, a superferry able to carry 2,290 passengers, 650 cars and 100 freight vehicles.*
SOURCE: *P&O European Ferries.*

Ferry companies have already discovered that speed through the ports is also becoming a major issue with travellers. There can be long hold-ups at peak times while waiting to board Le Shuttle through the Tunnel, and Le Shuttle trains are not timetabled. On the other hand, ferry passengers can turn up for a timetabled sailing (the official check-in time is just 20 minutes beforehand – see Figure 4.4), relax on board, buy their duty-frees and tax-free goods in the extensive shops and enjoy a meal.

In committing itself to total quality service as the basis for all its operations, P&O has adopted very high standards in customer-service training for its staff. All of its employees take part in a company training scheme 'Taking Service Forward' which is linked to NVQ. This has been shown to pay handsome dividends in terms both of staff morale and of the levels of responsibility which they assume. To expect the highest standards is to challenge an individual's commitment to delivering these, and this is the fundamental requirement of the company for its staff.

CASE STUDY: THE WHITE CLIFFS EXPERIENCE

Dover is an old sea port and has a long tradition of cross-Channel links, but until recently, it was not a tourist destination as such: people just passed through the town on their way to and from the Continent. During the construction of the Channel Tunnel, however, Dover District Council realised that the town itself should somehow benefit from the business the Tunnel would bring and should therefore seek a share in the economic prosperity which seemed likely. The Council realised that the Tunnel would cause the

FIGURE 4.3 *The American-style diner First Base is a popular haunt with young people on the P&O superferries.*
SOURCE: *P&O European Ferries.*

ferry companies to become more competitive by introducing new ships and a new infrastructure, and it had also heard of changes in emphasis on the part of the Dover Harbour Board. What could Dover itself do to benefit from these changes? What had the town got to offer as a tourist destination?

Dover has a long history stretching back to Roman times. Dover and its people have always been in contact with the Channel: they have made their living from it by providing a passage and defending its shores, and they still provide the coast guard and other services which make the Dover Straits safe. It is hardly surprising, then, that Dover District Council decided to invest in a high-quality facility which reflects the town's maritime heritage. Thus, the 'White Cliffs Experience' was constructed. This shows a magnificent panorama of the UK's history as seen through the eyes of the people who lived there; from the Celts and Romans to the wartime residents of Britain's 'Frontline Town'.

FIGURE 4.4 *P&O car passengers can expect a speedy service as they check in and a wait of only 20 minutes to board a timetabled ferry.*

So how did Dover decide on this attraction? In studies which were made in the late 1980s, the Council recognised that if its aim was to pull in private investment in the form of retail, commercial and leisure developments, a major catalyst would be required to convince investors that Dover 'meant business'. The Tunnel and the improvements at the port were one thing. Getting people into the town was another. The town had to provide something unique, exciting and substantial to draw people into what was not perceived to be a destination town. The town already possessed Dover Castle which welcomed over 200,000 visitors a year, and changes were planned for the Western Docks, but these would not of themselves meet the demands of the Council. A major flagship investment, aimed at developing a visitor product, raising the **market profile** and creating **investor confidence**, was required. However, with such a policy – that is, one of seeking to create a *market-led product* rather than to follow a *market-trends approach* – went intrinsic risks.

The decision was taken to create the White Cliffs Experience in the town centre as part of the heritage provision in Dover which also includes a museum, the castle and the town gaol (see Figure 4.5). Dover District Council also decided on a major refurbishment of many parts of the town centre, with attractive pedestrianised streets. The result is a major transformation. There are car parks and a coach drop-off point near the White Cliffs Experience in the centre of town. Other car parks and a coach park are situated within a short walking distance (see Figure 4.1). There is much attractive signposting to enable visitors, including many from abroad, to find their way around. There is a comprehensive local public-transport system linking the town centre with the car and coach parks, the railway station, the docks, the Tunnel and the other attractions which the town has to offer. There are also links with other Kent attractions, such as Canterbury. The new road and rail links to London and beyond are all seen as part of Dover's development as a tourist destination.

The success of the project has depended greatly on marketing. The whole image of the town, not just the White Cliffs Experience, had to be considered. People's perceptions of Dover had to be changed – a major undertaking (similar problems have had to be faced in ports on the other side of the Channel – in Calais, Boulogne and Dieppe, for example). However, Dover is already being marketed widely in France, Belgium and the Netherlands. The White Cliffs Experience is a success, and a model for others to follow.

FIGURE 4.5 *The White Cliffs Experience in the town centre of Dover. The Dover Museum is the white building on the left.*
SOURCE: *The White Cliffs Experience, Dover.*

ON THE CREST OF A WAVE? DEVELOPING DOVER'S LEISURE AND TOURISM INDUSTRIES

CASE STUDY: THE DOVER HARBOUR BOARD

The Dover Harbour Board (DHB) was established by Royal Charter in 1606 and entrusted with the administration, maintenance and improvement of the harbour. Subsequent statutes have amended the terms of the Charter but the principle remains the same, and the Board's present status is of seven members under a Chairman who is appointed by the Secretary of State for Transport.

The DHB derives its income from a number of sources, but mainly through the fees charged for the use of the port and its facilities. In recent years, numerous traffic records have been set for passengers, cars, coaches and lorries travelling on ferries, as well as for cruise-ship calls, visiting yachts and the use of the Dover Cargo Terminal which specialsises in the trade of fresh produce. The work of the DHB has also diversified towards a yacht-repair and chandlery business, as well as towards rescheduling the management of one of the most prestigious hotels which it owns in the town.

The reconstruction of the Dover Western Docks Marine Station as a cruise-liner terminal, completed in 1996, has cost £9 million, and will make the terminal one of the most modern embarkation ports in the world. The statistics shown in Figure 4.6 give some idea of the huge amount of traffic which uses the port each year. Figure 4.6 demonstrates significant increases in all sectors, and in 1995, the DHB accounted for 61% of all cars and 78% of all lorries which crossed the Channel. However, Figure 4.7 does show certain anomalies which we should consider. The Channel Tunnel is clearly making its presence felt on some of the figures, but is not yet operating at full capacity. The DHB is planning for the further impact of the Tunnel, and has decided to

FIGURE 4.6 *Annual traffic through the Port of Dover.*

Year	Passengers	Tourist cars	Coaches	Road haulage units
1970	5,051,751	836,667	12,938	83,277
1975	6,912,402	1,006,253	24,210	267,332
1985	13,783,840	1,575,281	117,669	798,376
1995	17,872,712	2,893,835	158,167	1,055,926

SOURCE: *Dover Harbour Board.*

FIGURE 4.7 *The Port of Dover – a statistical summary.*

	Port total		
	1995	**1994**	**% changes**
Passengers	17,872,712	19,125,645	−6.6
Cars	2,893,835	3,233,837	−10.5
Coaches	158,167	157,088	0.7
Road haulage vehicles	1,055,926	1,158,296	−8.8
Rail wagons	20,039	29,337	−31.7
Vessel entries			
Ferry	20,851	20,842	+0.0
Hovercraft	2,697	3,159	−14.6
Seacat	226	47	+380.9
General cargo	410	394	+4.1
Cruise	25	25	0.0
General cargo tonnes	609,763	588,447	3.6

SOURCE: *Dover Harbour Board.*

RECREATING THE GOLDEN AGE OF TRAVEL WITH THE NEW CRUISE TERMINAL AT DOVER

Dover Marine Station, once the most famous railway terminal outside of London, was the epicentre of a style of travel long forgotten. Before the era of the automobile and aeroplane the Western Docks and Dover Marine Station were the terminus for luxury continental passenger services and transatlantic cruise liners.

Heads of state and royalty frequently travelled this way to Europe. And from March 1996, you will be able to offer your customers the opportunity to step back in history and retrace the footsteps of King George V, Queen Mary, Winston Churchill and Lloyd George, to name but a few.

The quayside Marine Station is to be restored and refurbished into a cruise liner terminal. Steeped in nostalgia, this building will once again recreate the romance of that golden age of travel.

The terminal will be the first dedicated passenger facility to be built in the UK for several decades. A multi-million pound investment will offer you and your customers all the comforts of a modern purpose built terminal in a unique historic ambience, in a separate area of the port.

Passengers expect the highest quality on a cruise, and the Dover Cruise Terminal will enhance the travel experience. The latest security systems for people and their baggage, fast check-in facilities, baggage and stores handling, lounge areas, under-cover car parking and coach areas have all been included in the project specification.

Dover boasts an unrivalled position on the shipping lanes, fast motorway access to major airports, London and other tourist attractions. Added to this, Dover has its own magnificent White Cliffs and medieval castle.

The new Cruise Terminal offers an authentic, historical backdrop combined with modern day efficiency and luxury, which makes Dover a unique port for cruise line operators.

For further information and informed discussion of your operational requirements please contact: John Turgoose, General Manager (Shipping), Port of Dover, Harbour House, Dover, Kent CT17 9BU, UK. Tel: +44 (0) 1304 240400. Fax: +44 (0) 1304 240465.

TERMINAL LOCATION

BERTH FACILITIES

Length of berth	300 metres.
Depth of water	9.5 metres below Chart Datum.
Access	No restriction (24 hour operation).
Services	Pilotage, tugs, mooring, security and terminal facilities all under the direct management of the port.
Fendering	Yokahama fenders.

TERMINAL FACILITIES

Passenger walkway	Covered walkway adjustable between 10 metres and 19 metres above Chart Datum.
Reception areas	Ground floor check-in and security. Escalators, lift and stairways to first floor lounge seating 450.
Baggage handling	1,500 square metres of covered baggage handling area with additional covered area available by prior arrangement.
Parking	250 covered spaces adjacent to terminal. Over 25 coach bays adjacent to baggage check-in.
Disabled	All facilities "disabled-friendly".
Timescale	Opening March 1996.

DOVER

FIGURE 4.8 *A recent publication of the Dover Harbour Board to advertise its new cruise-liner terminal.*
SOURCE: *Dover Harbour Board.*

ON THE CREST OF A WAVE? DEVELOPING DOVER'S LEISURE AND TOURISM INDUSTRIES

seek out a new **market niche** which, hitherto, has only had a marginal effect on its income generation. The pamphlet shown in Figure 4.8 gives you some idea of the plan being made. Already in 1996, more than 100 cruise liners (see Figure 4.9) will commence or terminate their cruise programme in Dover – a four-fold increase in just one year – and so far, four major cruise lines have decided to commence and end a majority of their cruises at the new terminal (see Figures 4.8 and 4.10) in Dover.

In addition to the development of the liner business, the DHB is also expanding the 250-berth yachting marina. The coach interchange, which allows for the consolidation of coach tours to various destinations in Europe for people arriving in Dover in vehicles from all over the UK, is another major growth area.

FIGURE 4.9 *The huge Cunard cruise liner Vistafjord is nudged into Dover Harbour.*
SOURCE: *Dover Harbour Board.*

FIGURE 4.10 *The newly refurbished interior of the former Western Dock Railway Station at Dover, now an ultra-modern cruise-liner terminal.*
SOURCE: *Dover Harbour Board.*

Key Skills Hint: Communication

Using images in a presentation

Flip charts, videos, posters, blackboards/white-boards, slides, overhead-projector transparencies, printed hand-outs – all are visual aids that facilitate the use of images within an oral presentation. Your choice and subsequent use of images need to be carefully thought out to have the maximum impact. Bear the following points in mind when planning your presentation:

- Is the image necessary? Ensure that an image, if used, will get the message over better than by other means. Don't include images just because you think it is expected
- Which image could you use? You may need to choose between different styles of graph, diagram, map, chart, picture and photo

- What is the best way to present the image? Which visual aid will illustrate the information in the clearest and most eye-catching way?
- Be prepared to introduce each image in your presentation. Always give each illustration a title plus supporting information in the form of labels, a key, a scale or captions as necessary
- Keep illustrations simple – don't include too much information on one image for your audience to easily understand. Bullet points are useful 'shorthand' for points you are making in your presentation
- Images may be used to introduce topics or alternatively to provide a summary of the points you have made in your presentation.

TASK 17

The following is an integrated task which will need much careful preparation, implementation and evaluation.

- Your task is to consider the overall provision for either leisure or tourism in your locality
- You are to select up to five of the facilities available for research, and you are to ask the key question: what is the common issue which the organisations behind these facilities need to address? Note: in the investigation just completed on Dover, the common theme was the effect of the Channel Tunnel on future operations. You might select as your common theme a requirement that the town produce an overall sports and leisure strategy with the aim of improving provision for certain target groups. You might, on the other hand, identify a major resource in your area which seems at

the moment to be underutilised or neglected but which has obvious potential
- You are to seek the opinions of a wide range and valid cross-section of the local community, and to analyse your findings into a series of key questions for which you are then to seek strategic answers
- Decide how you are to publicise your intention to seek a public response to your findings – you might produce a leaflet or posters, or seek interviews on local radio, on TV, or in the local newspapers
- Map out your strategy for obtaining responses, and carefully plan to assign members of your group to specific tasks, aiming also to record, perhaps on video, samples of situations where data is being collected and feedback given
- You are to collate your responses in a

systematic way, aiming to transfer new data into a graphic or spreadsheet format. You need to end up with a clearly defined decision: have you been able to show that your locality would benefit from an overall systematic approach to the issue you have identified?

- Prepare a short, sharp oral presentation that could be given to key figures in your community. You should make clear what benefits you expect your project to bring. If costs are involved, you will need to analyse what these are and to suggest who might cover them.
- Carry out an evaluation of your findings and decide, in the light of experiences gained, which points you would bear in mind in any other similar in-depth investigation

You should aim to use Task 17 above as your own case study to which you can refer throughout your Advanced course in order to trace its development, monitor its progress and continually evaluate its potential. In this way, you will be investigating the leisure/tourism industry in your area through *personal involvement*. As a result, your studies will be extremely worthwhile, and will give you plenty of motivation to succeed in your work.

SECTION

5

Review of the Unit

By now, you should have acquired a real taste for the leisure and tourism industries. Unit 1 is about an overall introduction to your Advanced course, an opportunity for you to sample the structure and scale of products and services in these industries, tracing their development and investigating their impact on the environment and the community.

The case studies we have used have been chosen because they pick out some of the rich diversity of the industries. We have considered the roles played by private, international and national firms and organisations who help to ensure the smooth operations of the industry, and we have investigated the part played by public authorities in meeting their own responsibilities and delivering their own services.

How have you got on? We have challenged you to look at your own local situation through the case-study examples. You have first brainstormed which facilities exist in your area. Then, you have identified which organisation fits into which sector. You have probably then visited some of these organisations, talked to their staff and managers, discovered how they are run and come to a decision about their operational effectiveness. As a result, you will have become perhaps a little more critical about what you find around you, and certainly more observant of the issues with which your local facilities daily have to wrestle. You will also have drawn up your own agenda for further study, perhaps having decided to concentrate on a particular venue for more detailed investigation and study.

Advanced vocational courses do involve practically applied skills and practical experiences. We hope that your investigation of the leisure and tourism industries will lead you to develop the talents of working with others, keen observation and sensitivity towards the issues involved. Good luck in your future studies!

Useful Addresses

The addresses listed here appear in the same order as they are used in the text.

Office for National Statistics
Great George Street
London SW1P 3AQ

British Tourist Authority
Thames Tower
Black's Road
Hammersmith
London W6 9EL
Tel.: 0181 846 9000

Department of National Heritage
2–4 Cockspur Street
London
SW1Y 5DH
Tel.: 0171 211 6000

The Bluebell Railway
Sheffield Park Station
Nr. Uckfield
East Sussex TN22 3QL
Tel.: 01825 723777

Thomas Cook Group
45 Berkeley Street
London W1A 1EB
Tel.: 0171 408 4175

P&O European Ferries
Channel House
Channel View Road
Dover
Kent CT17 9TJ
Tel.: 01304 223000

European Passenger Service (Eurostar)
EPS House
Waterloo Station
London SE1 8SE
Tel.: 0345 881 881

Montagu Ventures Ltd (National Motor Museum)
Beaulieu
Brockenhurst
Hampshire SO42 7ZN
Tel.: 01590 612 345

USEFUL ADDRESSES

Kompan Ltd
3 Holdon Avenue
Bletchley
Milton Keynes MK1 1QU
Tel.: 01908 642466

Norfolk County Council
County Hall
Martineau Lane
Norwich NR1 2SG
Tel.: 01603 222206

The White Cliffs Experience
Market Square
Dover
Kent CT16 1PB
Tel.: 01304 210101

The Dover Harbour Board
Harbour House
Dover
Kent CT17 9BU
Tel.: 01304 240 400

Dover Tourist Information Centre
Town Wall Street
Dover
Kent CT16 1JR
Tel.: 01304 205108

Glossary

Administrative structures: how an organisation is run or organised, including the methods by which it is administered.

Built environment: the townscape, or a built-up area of interest, often containing properties of historical, architectural or archaeological interest.

Carrying capacity: how much pressure, usually from people, an area can carry or withstand before damage occurs.

Calming measures: methods used to control the speed and density of vehicles in sensitive areas.

Compulsory competitive tendering: a method which allows anyone to put in a bid to win a contract which they might also have the expertise to operate.

Culture: the artistic, historic, religious and linguistic features distinctive to a group of people.

Disposable income: the amount of money available for leisure and tourist pursuits after essential items, such as food, have been paid for.

Dual use: a method which allows facilities to be shared, perhaps between two or more organisations or between private and public users.

Heritage: historic buildings, artefacts and traditions distinctive to a group of people.

Honey pot site: popular and often overused leisure and tourism facilities.

Inbound tourism: the number of people visiting this country from abroad.

Interrelationships: the extent to which various aspects of each sector depend on and react with each other.

Investor confidence: attempts to convince investors, who put their money into a project, that their decision was the correct one.

Joint provision: the use of a facility by several interest groups, perhaps from both the private and public sectors.

Junk playgrounds: areas for children's play often made out of scrap (but safe) materials.

Leisure: pursuits and activities followed by people for enjoyment outside normal working hours.

Leisure society: the tendency for more and more people to be engaged in more and more leisure.

Listed properties: buildings which are protected by statute from being spoiled or altered in any way.

Market niche: a particular product offered for a particular reason or effect.

Market profile: an overview of the market and of how it responds to a need.

50

GLOSSARY

Market research: a process which involves surveys of potential or existing customers for a product or service.

Multiplier effect: the increase in local wealth and employment prospects caused by the development of leisure and tourism facilities or resources.

Official statistics: information provided from official sources, collected systematically by trained personnel.

Open system: an arrangement or organisation which is open-ended and subject to change and development, but constant in form.

Outbound tourism: the number of UK residents who travel abroad for tourism purposes.

Pedestrianisation: the process by which many high streets are given over entirely to *people*, with traffic and deliveries restricted to early morning or late at night.

Products and services: the output of a system, i.e. the production or the services offered.

Privately owned: facilities which are owned by individuals or shareholders who seek to profit from their interest and investment.

Price war: competition between rival organisations which can lead to reductions in price.

Publicly owned: facilities which are owned by public organisations and authorities, and are usually paid for out of tax revenues.

Recreation: the purposeful use of leisure time.

Scale: the extent to which an aspect of leisure or tourism is represented in an area or in the nation.

Sector: an aspect of the classification of leisure and tourism provision based on ownership and legal status.

Structure: how an aspect of a leisure or tourism facility is organised or managed.

Sustainable tourism: tourist activity which is designed to maintain or improve present conditions. Ecotourism emphasises low-tech, environmentally sensitive tourist activity.

Tourism: the temporary movement of people to destinations outside where they normally live and work.

Total Quality Management (TQM): a system devised in Japan to ensure the highest quality management in all aspects of operational activity.

Travel: the movement of people from one destination to another by various means.

Voluntary: involving organisations and activities run by volunteers and usually non-profit-making or charitable in status.

Index

active pastimes 2
administrative structures 3, 49
Anderson, Arthur 17

Beaulieu National Motor Museum 20, 21, 22, 23, 24, 28, 47
Bluebell Railway 12, 13, 30, 47
British Tourist Authority (BTA) 6, 32, 33, 47
built environment 28, 49
business travel 2, 3

calming measures 34, 49
carrying capacity 30, 49
Castle Hotel, Bramber 34
Castle Mall Shopping Centre 29
CD-ROM 19
Channel Tunnel 32, 34, 35, 37, 38, 44
Circular Note 17
compulsory competitive tendering 3, 49
Consumer Safety Unit 25
Cook, Thomas 16, 17
culture 2, 49

data collection techniques 7
Department of National Heritage 8, 47
Department of Trade and Industry 25
disposable income 2, 49
Dover Harbour Board 37, 41, 42, 43, 48
Dover Tourist Information Office 36, 48
Dover Town Council 38, 39, 40
dual use 3, 9, 49

economic impact 27, 28
environmental impact 27, 28
Environmental Impact Assessment 31
European Union 5, 25
Eurostar trains 19, 47

facts and figures 3, 4, 5, 6, 8, 32, 41
flow charts 15, 21, 22, 23

Golden Arrow 12

heritage 49
honey pot 19, 20, 27, 49

images 44
inbound tourism 4, 49
interrelationships 3, 49
interview techniques 7, 26
investor confidence 40, 49

joint provision 3, 9, 49
junk playgrounds 25, 49

Kompan A/S 24, 25, 26, 48

leisure 1, 2, 18, 24, 32, 49
Leisure Accident Surveillance System (LASS) 25
leisure society 28, 49
listed properties 34, 49

market niche 43, 49
market profile 40, 49
market research 15, 50
mission statement 23
Montagu of Beaulieu, Baron 20
Montagu Ventures Ltd 21, 22
multiplier effect 28, 50

National Lottery, The 9
Norfolk County Council 48

Office of National Statistics 4, 5, 6, 47, 50
open system 14, 50
outbound tourism 4, 50

park and ride 30
passive pastimes 2
pedestrianisation 30, 50
Peninsula and Oriental Steamship Navigation Company (P&O) 16, 17, 18, 37, 38, 39, 47

INDEX

play schemes   24, 25, 26
price war   37, 50
private sector   3, 9, 50
public sector   3, 8, 50

Quangos   8, 9
questionnaires   7

recreation   1, 18, 50

'Sea Breeze' guest house   11
Seaview Cafe   29
sector   50
services, products and   14, 18, 50
scale   50
Shaftesbury, Dorset   34

social impact   27, 28
Sterling of Plaistow, Baron   16
structure   50
Suez Canal   17
sustainable tourism   27, 28, 50

Thomas Cook   16, 17, 18, 47
Total Quality Management   15, 50
tourism   1, 2, 19, 32, 50
Tourism Charter   31, 34
travel   1, 19, 50

voluntary sector   3, 10, 50

White Cliffs Experience   37, 38, 39, 40, 48
Willcox, Brodie McGhie   17